CLIMATE CHANGE

I0177079

By Wendy Conway-Lamb

Library For All Ltd.

Library For All is an Australian non-profit organisation with a mission to make knowledge accessible to all via an innovative digital library solution. Visit us at libraryforall.org

Climate Change

First published 2021

Published by Library For All Ltd
Email: info@libraryforall.org
URL: libraryforall.org

This book was made possible by the generous support of the Education Cooperation Program and the University of Canberra.

Climate Change
Conway-Lamb, Wendy
ISBN: 978-1-922550-57-6
SKU01582

CLIMATE CHANGE

The climate is changing in Papua New Guinea.

This is Elma.

A big storm hit her house by the beach.

Her family is building a new home inland.

The climate is changing in Timor-Leste.

This is Fernando.

Heavy rain damaged his family's fields.

They are digging a canal to drain the flood water away.

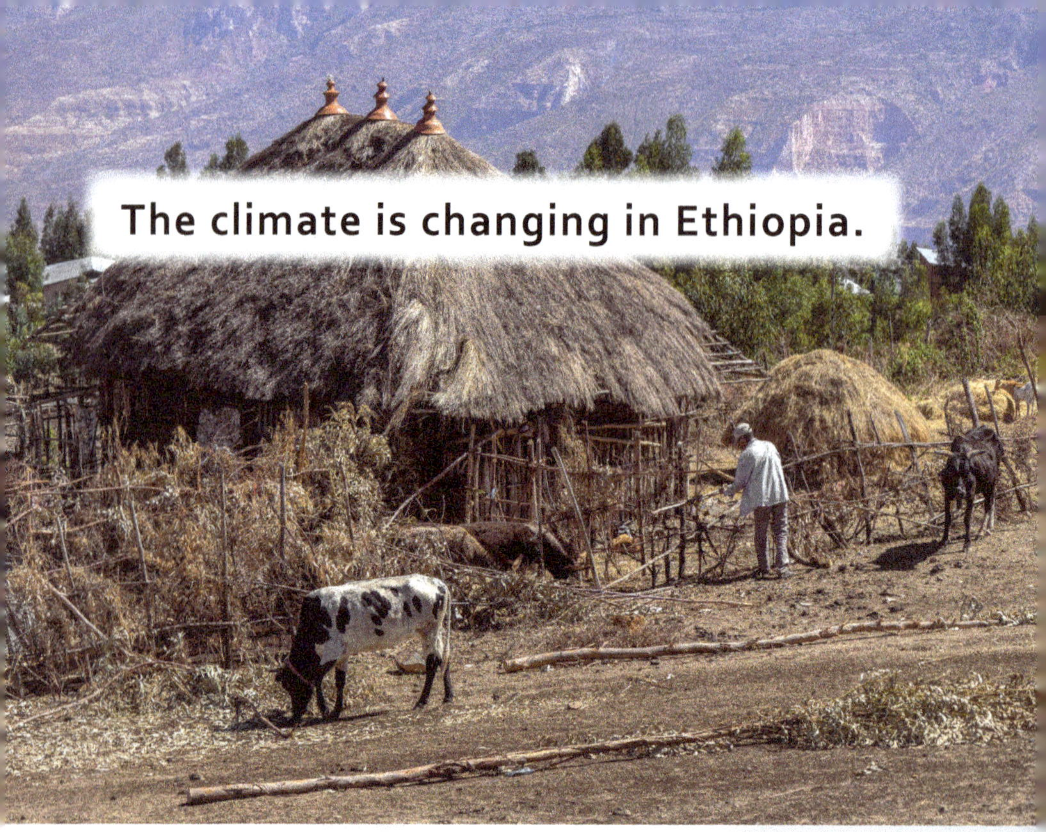

The climate is changing in Ethiopia.

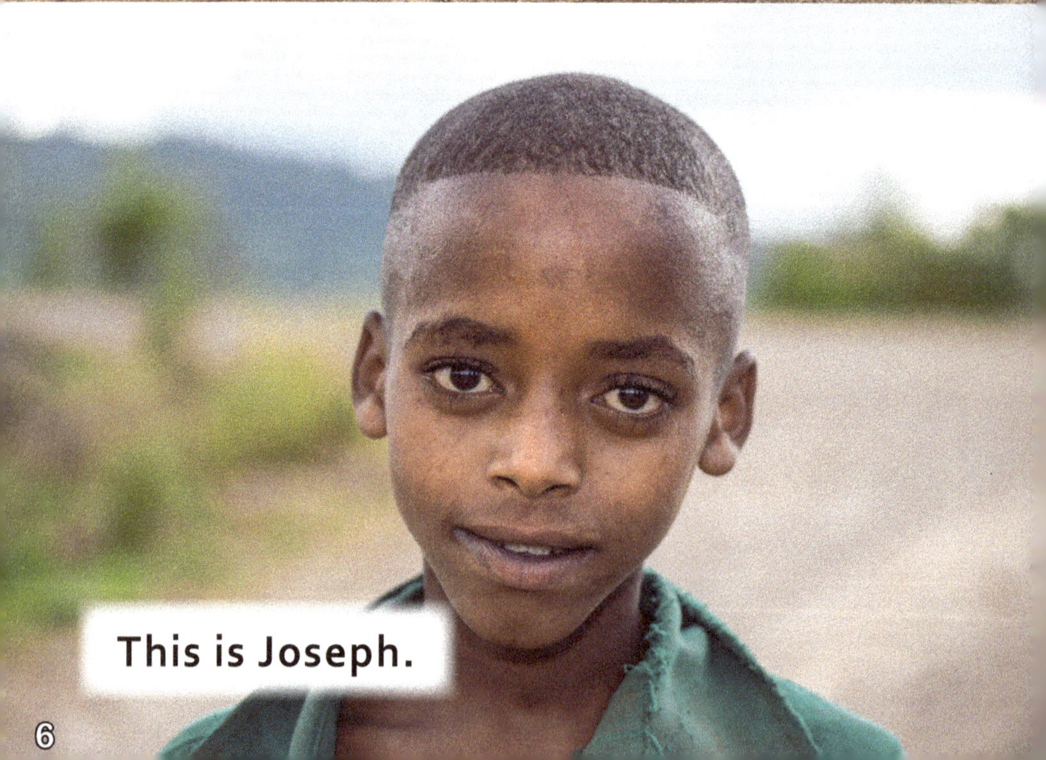

This is Joseph.

There is no rain so the crops will not grow.

His family is planting seeds that need less water.

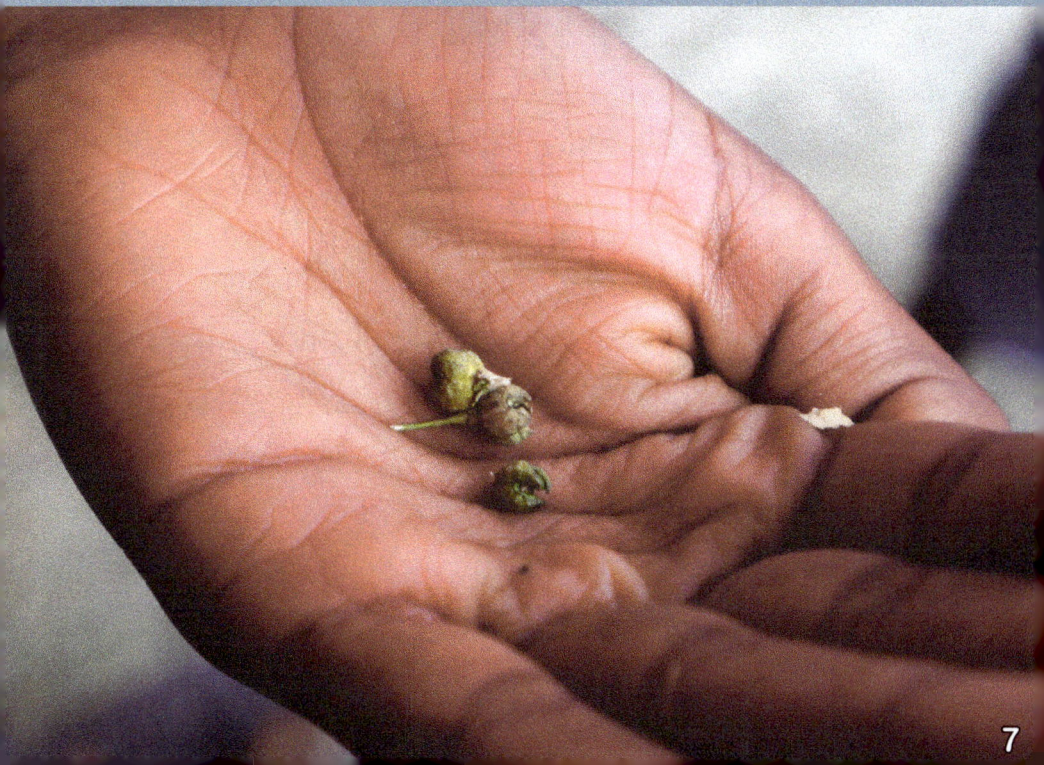

The climate is changing in Vietnam.

This is Huong.

Floods washed away the bridge over the river.

She is waiting for a boat to get to school.

The climate is changing in Australia.

This is David.

Bush fires have burned down his home.

His family is living in a tent.

The climate is changing in Tuvalu.

This is Selina.

The village well is full of salty sea water.

She is setting up a tank to collect rainwater to drink.

The climate is changing everywhere.

Elma, Fernando, Joseph, Huong, David and Selina are doing their best to adapt.

But why is the climate changing?

Factories are burning coal.

Cars and planes are burning petrol.

Forests are being cut down.

Our sky is filling with greenhouse gases.

They are like a blanket warming up our planet.

It changes the weather all over the world and the sea level is rising.

Can people fix this problem?

Yes! There are many ways to stop climate change.

We can plant lots of trees and protect our environment.

We can ask our governments to take more action.

We can make electricity from sun and wind power.

We can run cars on electricity instead of petrol.

Leaders from lots of countries have been talking about this at international meetings for decades.

Many people have started to make changes, but there is a lot more work to do.

If people and countries all work together we can slow down climate change and keep Elma, Fernando, Joseph, Huong, David and Selina safe.

Photo credits

Cover, title page, and pp. 16–17	Shutterstock.com/FloridaStock/ID: 702244504
p. 2 (top)	Shutterstock.com/ausnewsde/ID: 265819052
p. 2	Shutterstock.com/The Road Provides/ID: 1516361276
p. 3	Shutterstock.com/Michal Knitl/ID: 421136935
p. 4	Shutterstock.com/neenawat khenyothaa/ID: 1492571975
p. 5	Shutterstock.com/Jose_Matheus/ID: 1850619694
p. 6 (top)	Shutterstock.com/Artush/ID: 1423643837
p. 6	Shutterstock.com/Nick Fox/ID: 289781228
p. 7	Shutterstock.com/Stewart Innes/ID: 1636530190
p. 8	Shutterstock.com/GODONG-PHOTO/ID: 1828674917
p. 9	Shutterstock.com/NguyenQuocThang/ID: 758293153
p. 10 (top)	Shutterstock.com/JP Phillippe/ID: 1437869741
p. 10	Shutterstock.com/Daria Grebenchuk/ID: 428334106
p. 11	Shutterstock.com/Leah-Anne Thompson/ID: 160306139
p. 12 (top)	Shutterstock.com/Romaine W/ID: 1717607638
p. 12	Shutterstock.com/maloff/ID: 1305198187
p. 13	Shutterstock.com/donikz/ID: 1565266384
pp. 14–15	Shutterstock.com/Roschetzky Photography/ID: 766204174
pp. 18–19	Shuttertock.com/Alohaflaminggo/ID: 394298854
p. 20 (top)	Shutterstock.com/piyaset/ID: 1746515339
p. 20	Shutterstock.com/Alberto Menendez Cerveo/ID: 1663564561
p. 21 (top)	Shutterstock.com/Natee K Jindakum/ID: 1314541754
p. 21	Shutterstock.com/AnnGaysorn/ID: 1768250213
pp. 22–23	Shutterstock.com/Goami/ID: 466149698

You can use these questions to talk about this book with your family, friends and teachers.

What did you learn from this book?

Describe this book in one word. Funny? Scary? Colourful? Interesting?

How did this book make you feel when you finished reading it?

What was your favourite part of this book?

download our reader app
getlibraryforall.org

About the contributors

Library For All works with authors and illustrators from around the world to develop diverse, relevant, high quality stories for young readers. Visit libraryforall.org for the latest news on writers' workshop events, submission guidelines and other creative opportunities.

Did you enjoy this book?

We have hundreds more expertly curated original stories to choose from.

We work in partnership with authors, educators, cultural advisors, governments and NGOs to bring the joy of reading to children everywhere.

Did you know?

We create global impact in these fields by embracing the United Nations Sustainable Development Goals.

libraryforall.org

www.ingramcontent.com/pod-product-compliance
Lightning Source LLC
Chambersburg PA
CBHW040316050426
42452CB00018B/2871